TEACHERS AND TECHNOLOGY

---

*Understanding the Teacher's Perspective
of Technology*

Susan Louise Peterson

International Scholars Publications
Lanham · New York · Oxford

Library of Congress Cataloging-in-Publication Data

Peterson, Susan Louise, 1960
    Teachers and Technology : understanding the teacher's perspective of technology/ Susan Louise Peterson
        p. cm.
    Includes bibliographical references and index.
    ISBN 1-57309-378-5.Hardcover ; ISBN 157309-377-7.paper)
        1. Education technology—Psycholgical aspects. 2. Teachers—Attitudes.
        I. Title

LB1028.3.P45 1999
371.33—dc21   98-50334
                                                                    CIP

Editorial Inquiries:
International Scholars Publications
4720 Boston Way
Lanham, MD 20706

TEACHERS AND TECHNOLOGY

Dedicated to Alan,
who teaches me something new each day
about computer technology!

TABLE OF CONTENTS

FOREWORD

Teachers and Technology: Understanding the Teacher's Perspective of Technology - this book not only enlightens teachers, but points out problems with techno-phobia, lack of technical funds and priorities of schools regarding technology training. However, this book does not stop there. It also gives the reader a method of ideas and solutions.

Already, we see children with computer skills beyond their teachers. This happens because many children have better access to technology at home than at their school. Computers are the great equalizers in today's job market. What happens to those who do not get a chance to tap into this training? You will see more of what I see each day. Those losing jobs to more skilled workers.

Yes, I work in today's job market. I am an automation consultant, hired by companies to teach their employees. I started teaching technology 13 years ago. It was much simpler then, and people could learn at a slower method. Today, employers are not willing to spend the amount of money to educate an employee who has to start at the very beginning. They spend their training costs on those who already have a computer background. Technology learning is like learning mathematics. It builds upon prior experience. You can teach timetables to a child who already knows how to add, but try teaching timetables to a child who has no concept of numbers.

Children learn like the wind when it comes to computers, because they have no fear. Recently I purchased an interactive storytelling CD for my eight-year old daughter. While I was looking for the menu on how to begin the program, she just reached and clicked on an icon that looked like a paper with the corner folded down. When I asked how she knew to start the program, she said, "I wasn't sure, but on my other CDs, you click on different items on the screen, like trees, boats, animals, and something happens." Here, I am the expert and still looking for a familiar menu. That is how fast technology changes.

I know all children want to learn how to use a computer. Here in our grasp is an avenue for all children to learn, stand in line to learn, and yet our schools have not placed a priority on this great learning tool. These reasons and possible solutions are shown to you in this book.

Gina Novelle, author of *A New and Easy Way to Learn Windows 95* **and Automation Consultant, Compu-Teach, Las Vegas, Nevada.**

FOREWORD

For the average teacher, becoming proficient with technology advances and systems can be a difficult and frustrating experience. Even if desire and interest is prevalent, time is not. The average teacher's day consists of constant battles, challenges, changes, questions, answers, projects, exercises and confrontations. Their nights and weekends are spent cleaning up from the previous round of interactions and preparing for the next encounter. Learn how to use a desktop computer? When? Prepare a dynamic series of interactive computer programs that the students will love? How? Troubleshoot a malfunctioning hard drive? Yeah, right!

Dr. Susan Louise Peterson attacks this problem head-on by outlining short, concise steps that teachers, administrators and school districts can quickly and easily use to evaluate their technology education programs. This book does not attempt to solve all problems associated with technical training, but provides a starting point that can be used by education professionals to assess their level of technical expertise, understand their attitudes toward technology and evaluate the amount of technology required and available in each classroom or school.

Dr. Peterson provides tools and recommendations that will assist teachers in their quest to both learn and use technology. She suggests creative ways for developing technology-based criteria, implementing technology solutions, motivating student participation and phrasing technology reports and requests. School districts will still have difficult decisions to make concerning curriculum, budgets and equipment purchases, but they can use this book to begin the process and more importantly determine their goals, desires and needs in the technology arena.

Gregory Kreis, BS, MCSE, Director
Computer Skills Institute, Las Vegas, Nevada

PREFACE

I had been thinking about writing this book for several years. The lack of training for teachers in the technology area had really started to bother me. Daily I watched old broken down computers being wheeled around the schools. I observed a computer technology lab being closed up for a year because the school district was unable to find a computer teacher. I was watching the world of technology change so rapidly, but I was observing school districts responding slow to the change. I saw teachers resisting these technology changes because they did not have time or desire to learn these new skills. I wrote this book to explore some of the problem areas and ongoing issues for teachers using technology. It is meant to help understand the teacher's perspective of using technology. I am sure this book does not speak for every teacher, but there are some common concerns and problems that many teachers face in the technology realm.

One of the strengths many teachers have is the ability to take complicated ideas and concepts and put them into understandable terms that help their students. Teachers can be a wonderful and powerful resource for helping to spread technology, especially if they obtain the knowledge, technical skills and information to share with others. A teacher who is self confident and comfortable teaching technology can enlighten and enrich students on the technological changes that will impact our future. However, school districts and educational agencies must meet the challenges of helping teachers to grow and master technology skills, so they will be able to help their students toward a bright future in a technological world.

ACKNOWLEDGMENTS

My thanks to Dr. Robert West of International Scholars Publications for his support and encouragement. He has been very patient with my multiple submissions and still gets back to me in a timely manner.

I would also like to thank two professionals for reviewing the book who work in the area of teaching computer technology. First, I would like to give a big thanks to Gina Novelle, an automation consultant who dedicates her life to teaching adults and children on how to operate computers. She works hard to help frustrated adults and teachers find an easy and comfortable way to use the computer. Second, I would like to thank Gregory Kreis, Director of the Computer Skills Institute in Las Vegas, Nevada, for his comments on the book. Gregory is an expert in teaching computers and knows first hand the problems and concerns adults have in learning how to operate computers.

I want to thank a very special person, my husband Alan, for helping me prepare the manuscript. He has helped me in many ways to be more comfortable with computers and technology.

CHAPTER ONE

WHY TECHNOLOGY IS CONFUSING TO TEACHERS

The world of technology came to schools quickly and many teachers were confused when they saw a section in their curriculum guides on technology. They began to question their principals and school district administrators on how they were suppose to teach something they knew nothing about or had only minimum training. The principals and school administrators had difficulty answering many of the teacher's questions because they were just learning many of these technological advances themselves. Teachers remained even more confused as computer equipment, laser disc players and a variety of technology related equipment and materials were delivered to their schools. Some teachers jumped right in and took the challenge of learning how to operate these new gadgets. Other teachers never even plugged in the computers that were in their rooms and loudly exclaimed, "I do not know how to use it." Many teachers do not have a clear picture of what the area of technology means and how it can be used effectively as part of the school curriculum. They may be asked to teach it to students, but because teachers do not know what technology means, they only squeeze a short presentation into their lesson plans to cover themselves in case a state or federal education audit team visits their school. The rest of the technology curriculum guide will be skipped over by some teachers because they just do not have time and knowledge to teach the information to students. There is a need for schools to approach technology with great fervor and to help teachers become comfortable using it.

DEFINING TECHNOLOGY

Most teachers enjoy teaching subjects that they are familiar with and are comfortable in understanding. For example, some teachers have had years of college course work in teaching reading. They have had staff development training to learn strategies to help students learn to read. In addition, teachers have had a variety of inservice workshops to remind them of many of these reading techniques. A teacher who enjoys teaching reading usually does not use just one technique to teach a student to read. They have learned enough strategies to know that they will have to vary their techniques to help a class of students who have a variety of reading problems. However, when teachers are asked to teach technology as part of the curriculum, they may not have the same comfort level as they do in teaching reading. Some teachers are confused about the definition of technology. They are not sure what part of it to emphasize or what it really means to the students in their classes.

Teachers want a practical definition they can relate to in their own educational world. An engineer or a computer programmer may define technology by changing inputs to outputs, but this idea would be foreign to most teachers. School districts often have curriculum specialists who write the technology sections of these curriculum guides. The problem is that teachers often do not know how the school district defines technology. They are given a huge three-ring binder that is proudly displayed on top of the their filing cabinets. The teacher then continues with the rapid pace of the school year. The many tasks of displaying bulletin boards, completing report cards every six to nine weeks, writing lesson plans, preparing class materials, and dealing with the problems of students and parents take a toll on a teacher. I really do not think that most teachers do this on purpose, but they are creatures of habit and they have a certain routine of getting their classes organized. If technology is not emphasized as being important by principals and school district administrators, many teachers will avoid teaching technology and stick to subjects they are comfortable in sharing with their students. Without a practical definition of technology, teachers can not relate to students. The definition of technology for many teachers must be related to the mission or goals of the school district where they work.

THE IMPORTANCE OF TECHNOLOGY

Teachers have to see the importance of technology in their classrooms. They hear hype and jargon, but if they do not see how technology benefits the teachers and the students, they will lose interest in it. For example, several years ago, I attended a computer workshop on making grade spreadsheets. The person teaching the class made this process so complicated that the teachers started to laugh and make comments quietly to each other. I kept hearing little overtones like, "This is ridiculous because it takes hours to do this," or "I can do my grades faster by hand." Teachers are concerned with the time elements because they work long hours. Some teachers spend several hours after school organizing for the next day's class activities. A person observing at schools would see teachers taking home bags of materials to work on every evening and weekends. Teachers have to see the relevance of technology to be enthusiastic enough to teach it.

FEAR OF THE UNKNOWN

Another confusing thing for teachers with technology is the fear of the unknown. Teachers are asked to teach curriculum they do not know and understand. In most subject areas, teachers have had years of college work and experiences to share with students. In the technology realm, teachers have had to yield to students who are more knowledgeable of computers than they are. It is fearful for a teacher to teach a subject to students on up-to-date information. Some teachers become intimidated and threatened by the abundance of knowledge the students are bringing to their classes. It is obvious when this happens that school districts must see the value of getting professional and high quality training for teachers in the area of technological advances. If teachers are not up-to-date on the technology issues in our society, they can not help their students with a clear picture of the technological issues they will face in the future. Teachers must overcome their fears related to the technology.

BALANCING TECHNOLOGY WITH CURRICULUM

Teachers have one more thing to add to their curriculum with the addition of technology. This is a burden for teachers who are already dealing with time constraints. Teachers do not feel they have enough time to teach the areas they are now required to teach, so adding technology is a major stress for many of them. However, this stress can be relieved by training teachers to balance technology with the current curriculum they are teaching to their students. Some teachers may even teach elements of technology in core subject areas without even knowing it. Once teachers realize technology can easily be integrated into the subject areas, they are not as confused and frightened when it is mentioned in educational circles. Teachers are important in bringing technical information to the level a student can understand and use throughout his or her life. The role of the teacher as a practitioner for sharing technological information is crucial in helping to change the lives of children. If teachers overcome the confusion of technology, they will have the potential to be technological change-agents in our society. Technology must be balanced with the daily curriculum so teachers can help students to be prepared for the future. The curriculum can only be enhanced if teachers use technology to open new avenues for students.

TECHNOLOGY PROBLEM AREAS FOR TEACHERS

There are problem areas for teachers and schools when technology becomes a part of the school setting. Many of these technological problem areas need to be addressed in school districts.

1. Outdated Equipment

There are schools with tons of old, outdated computer equipment gathering dust in storage closets. One school I observed, made sure that every teacher in the school had a computer in his or her room. This sounded wonderful when the principal wrote a glowing report to the district administration on the wonderful technological advances at the school. The picture was somewhat different from the teacher's perspective. Teachers had computers with broken parts, missing cords and defective software. Yes, each teacher had a computer in his or her classroom, but the computers were useless because they were idle and not functional for the teachers to use with students. Teachers spend hundreds of dollars out of their salaries to buy school supplies each year. They rarely want to spend any additional money to buy parts and software for out dated computers.

2. Lack of Available Computers and Equipment

Some school districts go to elaborate lengths to make sure each classroom is wired for computer hook-ups. However, that does not mean every classroom has a computer. Teachers and school specialists may even question if a single computer should serve thirty to forty students in a classroom. I spoke with an elementary school librarian who felt computers helped students look up information in the library. She said the problem was having only one computer. It took a long time for each student to look up information on books they wanted to check out of the library. The other students would get restless until they had a turn on the computer. The old card catalogues had been discarded so the computer was the only resource the students had to look up the reference information.

When there is only one computer in a classroom, it is not always used by the students. Teachers will use the computer for their organizational and management needs. Teachers also use computers for school newsletters, grade reports, and notes to parents. A classroom may contain a computer, but is does not mean it is accessible to students for learning activities and exchanging information.

3. Lack of Technological Personnel to Assist Teachers

Teachers will admit they are behind the times in the technological world. Many teachers feel they need more training in computers and technology. However, in many school districts, technology strategist positions go vacant for years. If computer professionals are hired to work with teachers and students, they may be responsible for three or four schools. Each school may have a computer specialist come to their campus one day a week. As a result, only a limited amount of technological information is shared with students and teachers.

The problem is further complicated by the fact that computer and technology specialists are in great demand and can earn higher salaries than school districts are willing to pay. When technology specialists can double their salaries apart from education, schools face difficulty in recruiting qualified individuals to operate their technology centers. I reviewed a grant proposal providing computer training for teachers. The teachers were to be paid twenty dollars an hour to attend a training workshop for several weeks. I asked the proposal writer how much he would pay the computer specialist to teach the workshop. He replied, "About twenty dollars an hour." I thought it was ironic the specialist was going to train the teachers and be paid the same amount as the teachers attending the workshop. I began to wonder if any computer and technological specialist would take the teaching position if the grant was funded.

4. Lack of Inservice Training on Technology

I can honestly say that during my seven years of teaching in public elementary schools, I have only attended one required training session on technology. It was a short one hour presentation geared toward using technology in science lessons. The presentation on technology was interesting, but not long enough to see the whole picture. Many teachers have no hands on training in the area of technology, but are asked and required to teach it in their curriculum. Because teachers are unfamiliar with technology, they either totally avoid it or make excuses for not having time during the school year. In many cases, teachers receive training on learning strategies and learning styles, but not on technology.

There are teachers who receive limited training on computers. Teachers may have had experience working on Apple computers, while others work only on IBM compatible computers. They may take courses on developing spreadsheets or word processing documents on a computer. Many teachers then forget the information they learn in training because it is not reinforced when they return to their schools. If teachers do not have computers in their classrooms, computer information learned in workshops becomes irrelevant. It is important to realize that not all schools have access to the Internet. Some teachers will say they "know computers," but once you talk to them, you find out they have word processing skills and have never used the Internet.

Teachers must receive training that is consistent to the needs of their schools. If teachers are trained to operate equipment that is available in their schools, it will help prepare them for further technology training. Many teachers are totally unaware of the technology that is available in their schools. Once teachers become aware of this technology, they need to be inserviced on ways to use this information to enlighten themselves and their students. Technology inservice training for teachers must be arranged to fit the teacher's busy and hectic schedule.

5. Dealing With Student Abuse of Technology

The teacher's limited knowledge of technology also hinders their ability to spot student abuse of technology equipment. For example, a teacher who supervises a computer lab does not always realize students may be abusing the computers. It is not uncommon for a student to change keyboard typing keys or delete important system software files. The teacher and student in the next class may not be able to figure out what is wrong with the computer. Repair technicians may discover someone has poured glitter or glue into the computer. Students have been known to spill drinks on keyboards and scratch computer screens. One teacher found chewing gum in the disk drive. Water can also creep into computers causing a variety of problems. Students may erase important commands and system files that require a reinstall of the software. Teachers who supervise students working on computers need training on how to spot equipment abuses when students operate technology equipment.

6. Technology Needs of At-Risk Students

I taught at an inner city at-risk school for five years and have made many observations of students working with technology. It is interesting to compare impoverished at-risk students with children of parents working in professional positions. In middle class America, many students with parents in professional occupations use computers at home. These students are able to research topics and find up-to-date information on class projects. At-risk students often do not have this kind of support. Many of these students do not have computers in their homes. If computer labs are closed or limited in use because of shortages of money or the inability to hire a technology specialist, at-risk students will get virtually little or no computer training at home or at school. There is a great need to provide extra support in the technological areas for these at-risk students They need to be aware of technology and how it will have an impact on their future. In addition, students need to gain an awareness of technology in the occupations they are planning to enter.

7. Time Constraints for Teachers

Some schools provide computers in classrooms because they want teachers to learn how to use them. The thought behind this gesture is if teachers learn to operate a computer, they will be more excited about teaching and helping the students. However, many teachers are so busy during the school day with other activities, they hardly have a minute to sit down and learn computer skills. These teachers have a computer in their rooms, but they do not have time to use it. A few schools allow teachers to check out a computer and take it home for a semester or even a year. These teachers tend to have more time to become familiar with computer technology and the whole world of information exchange. Once they see the value and the mass amounts of information they can use to enrich their class lessons, they can enlighten students and become excited about teaching technology. Unfortunately, I have only seen a computer loan program for teachers in very few schools. Teachers often feel overworked and stressed by the demands of the school setting, and face time constraints in learning computer technology.

8. Technology Jargon

Teachers, like other professionals, struggle with understanding all the technology jargon that is floating around our world. A teacher goes to buy a computer and he or she may become intimidated as the computer salesperson bogs them down with technology jargon. Teachers become frustrated because they do not know the questions to ask to buy a computer or software for use in a home or school setting. Some teachers feel that they do not need to know all the inner workings of the computer to buy one. They do not have time because of class preparations and lesson plans to become computer experts. There are teachers who want to know the basics of how to run a computer and use it for students. Teachers need assistance in becoming familiar with the jargon that is used in technology circles. They also need to learn technology vocabulary words so they may encourage students.

9. Technology Support Needed for Teachers

Many technology problems can be addressed by creating technology support programs in the schools. For example, school personnel administrators need to conduct massive recruiting efforts to find qualified technological specialists to assist teachers. Newer equipment can be ordered, and outdated equipment can be cleaned out of the storage rooms and discarded. School districts can plan inservice programs and workshops for teachers on how to identify student abuse of equipment. Teachers should be given release time for developing skills. Grant proposals can be developed to provide additional opportunities for at-risk students to work with technology. Support can be provided to teachers, students and schools to prepare students for their role in the technology of the future.

ONGOING ISSUES FOR TEACHERS ON TECHNOLOGY USE

There are many ongoing issues challenging teachers in the use of technology. Some of these technological issues will be addressed in the following items:

1. Different Levels of Technology Expertise

It does not matter which school you visit, you will always find teachers with different levels of technological expertise. Someone conducted a computer technology survey of teachers at my school. Amazingly, half of the teachers felt they were at an intermediate level of computer knowledge, while the others felt they were at an introductory level. This presented a perfect opportunity to pair teachers as partners for sharing and exchanging technology information. Students are paired together for a variety of class activities, and it seems to work successfully for information exchange in the classroom. The same strategy can work for teachers because they are at different ability levels related to computer technology. The pairing of teachers with varying technology ability levels needs to change yearly as teachers transfer or are hired by the district.

Most schools usually informally identify at least one teacher or staff member who becomes the resident "technology expert." However, the school "technology expert" can get stressed out as other teachers are asking him or her questions and constantly bringing projects to the expert for help and assistance. It is kind of like the old adage that you do not tell people you can "type, sew or do taxes," because they will be at your door for help. Some teachers do not let others know of their technological knowledge because they know it means extra work and responsibilities.

2. Sequence Teacher Technology Training

Technology training for teachers should occur in a sequence that is consistent and useful. Much of the technology training teachers receive is delivered in bits and pieces. It is often the odds and ends of materials from earlier periods of technology information. Worse, teachers sometimes hear the same workshops several times. School districts must develop timelines and action plans so teachers can build on previous technology experience. A consistent, well-planned program of training in technology will strengthen self-confidence and skills useful in areas of technology. When teachers feel positive and confident about technology, they show a zest for it to their students. The instructors of technology inservice workshops must have an organized program that can be sequenced with the teachers previous technology experiences.

3. Training with New Techniques

Teacher technology training must be ongoing because of the constantly new products on the market. Teachers not only must update their skills, but they must learn new procedures and steps for operating the latest equipment. This is hard for many teachers who still use older, slower equipment in their classrooms.

4. Teachers Exchanging Information

The whole idea of a technology surge in our world occurred with advancements in how we exchanged information with each other. Universities connected by computer technology and up-to-date research share information at the touch of a few keys on the keyboard. This idea of exchanging information was shared with those in the public school environment. Teachers can share information on grant proposals they developed for projects. Teachers can now be connected to schools from other countries, and students can use computer technology to learn about other cultures. On a local level, teachers at different schools can team together for projects and field trips to student events. This technology is available, but not all schools and teachers are using it. Schools have varying technological resources. A number of teachers lack the training and skills necessary to connect with other schools. As a result, teachers miss opportunities to exchange information and ideas through the means of technology.

5. Futurology Training for Teachers

Most teacher education programs in universities do not include course work on futurology for teachers. If teachers are to properly understand the role of technology in the lives of their students, they must become familiar with understanding the future of technology. If teachers become aware of the fast pace of information, they will be able to assist their students in keeping up with the changing nature of technology. Teachers must also help students make informed and reasonable choices related to technological information presented to them on a daily basis. Teachers need information on current and future trends. In addition, teachers must help students explore the misuses and consequences of technology use. Coursework in futurology is desperately needed in teacher education programs. Inservice workshops are needed for experienced teachers to stay informed on futurology issues. It is a different world than twenty years ago and experienced teachers need futurology training in educational programs at college.

CHAPTER TWO

WHAT DOES TECHNOLOGY MEAN TO TEACHERS?

In order to facilitate teacher ideas about technology the following prompts are provided. Teachers are to complete the prompts and write a few sentences expressing their views and ideas about technology. These prompts are developed for teachers to write their opinions and then explore orally how they look at technology. A good follow-up activity is to form small groups so teachers can exchange their ideas.

1. **Technology means...**

2. **I use technology when I teach…**

3. **Technology frustrates me when…**

4. **One benefit of technology is…**

5. **Technology confuses me when…**

6. **Technology improves...**

7. **A strength of technology in our school is...**

8. **Technology in our school is monitored by...**

9. **A weakness of technology in our school is...**

10. Students enjoy using technology to...

11. The best technological resource in our school is...

12. My favorite aspect of technology is...

13. Parents can be involved in the school technology activities by...

14. **Change in technology causes me to...**

15. **The school technology specialist should...**

16. **Technology can be integrated with...**

17. **Technology resource information is housed in...**

18. **The school technology specialist is responsible for...**

19. **The principal views technology as...**

20. **As a teacher, I feel technology is important to...**

21. **Technology has improved my teaching by...**

22. **Technology is successful at our school because...**

23. **The problem with technology is...**

24. **A strategy to incorporate technology in our school would be...**

25. **The goal of technology is...**

26. The reason teachers need technology is...

27. A good technology activity for students would be...

28. Technology should be a priority area because...

29. Technology burdens me because...

30. **I observe students using technology to…**

31. **Technology enhances learning by…**

32. **A technology timeline would help teachers to…**

33. **Technology is a tool for students to…**

34. My favorite technological gadget is…

35. Technological equipment in my school is…

36. Technology sparks interest in students when…

37. I incorporate technology in the curriculum when…

38. Technology has caused me to rethink my ideas about...

39. The main problem students have with technology is ...

40. Technology causes me anxiety when...

41. The thing I least understand about technology is...

42. Students view technology with a sense of...

43. I apply technology in the curriculum by...

44. An example of technology use in our school is...

45. Technology has caused me to modify my teaching by...

46. The technology program at our school lingers because...

47. Students rind technology interesting because it...

48. Technology complements the curriculum because...

49. The value of technology is...

50. Technology will be a success if teachers will...

51. A good method for teaching technology is...

52. A technology unit should include...

53. The objective of technology in the classroom is...

54. Teachers need technology help with...

55. Technology facilitates learning by...

56. The role of teachers in technology is...

57. I associate technology with...

58. Teacher technology use can be evaluated by...

59. Technology generates new ideas for students because...

60. I find technology perplexing because...

61. I include technology in my lesson plans by...

62. **The limitations of technology are…**

63. **Technology can accelerate learning by…**

64. **I would compare technology with…**

65. **Technology is integrated in the content areas through…**

66. My best teaching experience with technology was...

67. One criticism I have about technology is...

68. Technological support is needed for teachers because...

69. Teachers defend the use of technology because...

70. **Technology influences students to…**

71. **Students gain technology skills by…**

72. **Students need more technology equipment to…**

73. **Technology training should be provided for teachers because…**

74. Technology in schools is intended to...

75. The greatest thing about technology in schools is...

76. Teachers connect technology with...

77. Technology contributes to...

78. Technology demonstrations would help teachers to...

79. Technology accents the curriculum by...

80. Teachers are attempting to use technology for...

81. The aim of technology should be related to...

82. **Technology could be interacted with...**

83. **The future of technology in our school is...**

84. **A technology grant proposal for our school should include...**

85. **I would describe the technology use at our school as...**

86. **An important point about technology is...**

87. **Technology assists teachers by...**

88. **Teachers need technology reports on...**

89. **Students abuse technology when they...**

90. **The school technology lab assists teachers by...**

91. **The quality of the technology program at our school is...**

92. **My expectation for technology in our school is...**

93. **Technology saves time for teachers by...**

94. The subject matter of technology should include...

95. The school technology lab should be redesigned to include...

96. Technology use could be promoted in our school by...

97. Parent involvement in technology is limited because...

98. School technology use can be evaluated by...

99. The emphasis of technology in the schools should be on...

100. Funding for technology in the schools seems to be...

CHAPTER THREE

PLANNING TEACHER TECHNOLOGY INSERVICE TRAINING

This chapter is written to help school districts with planning a teacher technology inservice training workshop. The workshop is designed as a starting point to introduce teachers to technology that is now part of the school curriculum. Each school district may have unique needs, so the information may have to be adapted or modified to each school's situation or circumstances. A variety of handouts have been developed to help teachers increase their understanding and awareness of technology and its use in schools. The teacher technology workshop can be used with teachers on several levels:

1. Introductory Level

The workshop can be used to introduce teachers to the definition and meaning of technology that is part of the school environment.

2. Intermediate Level

Teachers with more advanced technology skills can benefit from reinforcement of skills by the exchange of information that teachers share with each other during the workshop.

3. Expertise Level

Teachers who have a high level of technology skill can enrich their experiences through this workshop. They will find helpful information as they become master technology teachers and assist and mentor other teachers in their schools.

TEACHERS AND

TECHNOLOGY

Teaching Sequence for Teacher Technology Training

1) Explore the definition of technology with teachers
   - Share five ways teachers define technology
   - Have teachers write their definition of technology
   - Evaluate the school or district's definition of technology
   - Examine the many different aspects that technology entails for teachers

2) Benefits for teachers and students by the use of technology
   - Explore the four ways students benefit from the use of technology
   - Prioritize reasons for using computer technology in the classroom and discuss with colleagues
   - Review Internet information for teachers and students

3) Examine ways to balance technology with the curriculum
   - Discuss the handout balancing technology with the curriculum
   - Brainstorm ten ways to incorporate technology in the curriculum and share ideas in small groups

4) Inventory and discuss technology equipment and ability level
   - Inventory technology equipment and have teachers go to their rooms and inventory technology related equipment
   - Fill out and discuss the teacher ability level for working with technology equipment

5) Discuss ways teachers can encourage students to use technology

6) Select a teacher technology team and discuss the tasks of the team

7) Discuss ways to reward students for technology use

8) End the teacher technology inservice on a positive note by sharing the tips for a successful school technology program

FIVE WAYS TEACHERS DEFINE TECHNOLOGY

Technology Means Computers

There are teachers who would say that being good at technology means that you can operate a computer. Some teachers even think that if they type fast or know word processing programs, they are technology experts.

Technology Means Electronics and New Gadgets

These teachers think that being good in technology means that they can operate the VCR, pager, CD player, cell phone, and all the other new gadgets that appear daily.

Technology Means Finding Uses for Things

Teachers in this category see technology as the ability to find other uses for household items and different things in our society.

Technology Means Creating New Things

These teachers encourage students to take items and create new things that will help improve society.

Technology Means Understanding How Things Work

Teachers in this area like to tear things apart and encourage students to understand what makes things work.

DEFINE TECHNOLOGY

1) Write your definition of the word technology.

2) What is your school's definition of technology?

3) Once you have answered the above questions, pair yourself with another teacher to compare your answers.

Different Aspects of Technology

Technology can be defined in many ways because it entails a variety of aspects for teachers.

→**Understanding people and materials**

→**Application and use of equipment**

→**Organizing Knowledge**

→**Evaluating Learning**

→**Exchanging Information**

→**Designing and Repairing Materials and Equipment**

FOUR WAYS STUDENTS BENEFIT FROM THE USE OF TECHNOLOGY

1) Technology activities can bring the curriculum and printed word alive.

It is really an exciting time for students to learn about technology, because they have an opportunity to use hands-on information in activities that are fun and enlightening.

2) Technology has become a practical part of our lives.

Even though some people resist it, they still must adapt their lives to technology. Fast food restaurants may require job applicants to fill out an application on a computer. Some driver license exams are given on a computer screen.

3) Technology allows information to be shared in a broader sense.

A student researching a topic for a term paper can access information from colleges and universities, medical schools and research centers from around the world.

4) Technology has a changing nature.

Teachers have a great opportunity to share with students how technology can change their lives. They can explore how changes in technology impact transportation, medical care, engineering, and a variety of other areas in our world.

Prioritize Reasons for Using Computer Technology in the Classroom

Rank the following items on a scale from 1 to 10. Number 1 will be the most important reason for using computer technology in the classroom and 10 will be the least important reason.

_____ Obtaining information for class lessons

_____ Record keeping for class attendance and grades

_____ Keeping lesson plans

_____ Publishing and displaying student work

_____ Sharing and exchanging information with colleagues

_____ Student use for class projects

_____ Writing teacher newsletters and parent notes

_____ Student use in playing education games for enrichment

_____ Researching topics for advanced college study

_____ Student use for basic typing and word processing skill development

Internet Information That Would Help Teachers

⇒**Science and math reports**

⇒**Research sources**

⇒**Travel guides**

⇒**Lyrics for songs**

⇒**Weather information**

⇒**Games and jokes**

⇒**Historical events**

⇒**News items**

⇒**Graphics**

⇒**Animal information**

⇒**Movie and book reviews**

⇒**Pictures and illustrations**

This list is only a small part of what the Internet has to offer teachers. There are a million more resources available for teachers and school personnel.

Topics Students Might Want to Research on the Internet

→ Animal topics

→ Foreign languages

→ Government addresses

→ Available scholarships

→ Art collections

→ Museum information

→ Environmental issues

→ Music and theater resources

→ Newspaper stories

→ Sporting events

→ Space and planet topics

→ Geography information

Technology Skills That Can Help Students

* Making comparisons

* Locating information

* Following directions

* Describing a process

* Technology vocabulary

* Creating maps and models

* Identifying symbols

* Graphing data

* Contrasting items

* Reading a blueprint

* Repairing objects

* Building from scratch

Balancing Technology with the Curriculum

TEACHERS CAN USE TECHNOLOGY WHEN THEY TEACH ABOUT:

◊ Planning events

◊ Conducting experiments

◊ Solving problems

◊ Brainstorming ideas

◊ Designing something new

◊ Research and library skills

◊ Different cultures

◊ Listening skills

◊ Creative writing

◊ Inventions

◊ Exploring surroundings

Brainstorm Session

List 10 Ways You Can Incorporate Technology in Your Curriculum. Share Your Ideas in Small Groups.

1.

2.

3.

4.

5.

6.

7.

8.

9.

10.

School Technology Inventory

Conduct a school technology inventory in your classroom by checking technology related equipment and assessing the condition of the equipment.

Check the condition of the equipment

Equipment	How many?	Good	Repair	Discard
computers				
laser disc player				
scanner				
digital camera				
CD player				
VCR				
television				
radio				
satellite receiver				
CDI player				
fax machine				
2 way radio				
cellular phone				
pager				
zip drive				
tape player				
film projector				
overhead				
other				

Teacher Ability Level for Working with Technology Equipment

Check your ability level for working with the technology equipment listed below:

	I know how to operate this equipment.	I have limited knowledge about this equipment.	I do not know how to operate this equipment.
computers	_____	_____	_____
laser disc player	_____	_____	_____
scanner	_____	_____	_____
digital camera	_____	_____	_____
CD player	_____	_____	_____
VCR	_____	_____	_____
television	_____	_____	_____
radio	_____	_____	_____
satellite receiver	_____	_____	_____
CDI player	_____	_____	_____
fax machine	_____	_____	_____
2 way radio	_____	_____	_____
cellular phone	_____	_____	_____
pager	_____	_____	_____
zip drive	_____	_____	_____
tape player	_____	_____	_____
film projector	_____	_____	_____
overhead	_____	_____	_____
other	_____	_____	_____

Ways Teachers Can Encourage Students To Use Technology

1) Role model the proper use and care of technology equipment

2) Provide students opportunities to work with different technology equipment

3) Introduce a technology vocabulary word each day

4) Assign technology tasks to students each week

5) Provide hands-on experience with technology for students

6) Let students explore new gadgets and how they work

7) Encourage students to bring small technology devices for show and tell

8) Allow students to use the classroom technology equipment

9) Give students a box of items and ask them to create or design a technology device

10) Provide technology related materials and reports for students to review and critique

List five things you could do to encourage the use of technology with your students.

1.

2.

3.

4.

5.

Tasks of a Teacher Technology Team

1) Organize technology inservice training for teachers and other staff members

2) Develop a school technology handbook

3) Involve parents in school technology activities

4) Provide teachers with articles and information on new technological development

5) Prepare a yearly report of technology progress in the school

Rewarding Students for Technology Use

The following projects could be used to reward students for technology use:

1) Have the students redesign the school with modern technology, and reward outstanding designs.

2) Provide a contest for students to build a model of their community. Emphasize improving the community with the use of technology. Prizes will be given to students with the best models.

3) Plan a map designing activity for students. Students can use various technology equipment to design a map of the school. The students making the best use of technology for their maps will receive incentives.

4) Challenge the students with technology problem solving activities. Students must figure out how to solve the problem with some form of technology. Gift certificates awarded to all students who made an effort.

Tips for a Successful School Technology Program

* Plan technology themes and events before the school year so teachers will know what to expect.

* Review the school's technology objectives with teachers at a technology inservice workshop during the first week of the new school year.

* Pair teachers with different levels of technology expertise as partners, and complete a technology project.

* Develop a technology reference section in the school library for teachers and staff.

* Share positive technology experiences of students and teachers at staff meetings.

* Encourage positive attitudes among teachers toward technological change.

CHAPTER FOUR

TEACHER TECHNOLOGICAL PHRASES

The following is a list of some technological phrases teachers can use in writing reports or developing grant proposals in the technology area:

1. technology can be compared to
2. brainstorming helped the students understand technology
3. the students were thrilled by the new technology
4. the technology was questioned by the students
5. students spotted problems in the technology assignment
6. technology involves the organization of
7. the focus of technology is to
8. each technology activity had a purpose
9. students selected technology topics for projects
10. the school developed a technology plan
11. questioning was part of the technology activity
12. technology was illustrated by
13. the technology team submitted a
14. students gave responses to the technology projects
15. the technology projects were critiqued by
16. each classroom had a technology assignment
17. the school had a technology theme
18. the teacher attended a technology conference

19. technology issues were clarified by

20. technology assignments were submitted to

21. technology was a high priority item

22. the school emphasized technology by

23. technology was introduced in stages

24. the technology conference was helpful

25. students attended the technology conference

26. students wrote about their technological experiences

27. the strength of the technology program was

28. the technology program was weak in

29. an action plan was submitted by the technology department

30. the technology committee developed a handbook for

31. a criticism of technology is

32. technology opened the dialogue between

33. the technology presentation was organized

34. the teacher detailed the steps of the technology plan

35. teachers teamed together to address technology issues

36. the technology program was improved by

37. the school made an effort to support technology

38. the technology report was summarized by

39. the school analyzed the technology being used

40. the technology program was explained to teachers

41. a technology display was placed in the hallway

42. students created computer technology programs

43. students selected one aspect of technology to discuss

44. technology use improved in the school

45. technology experiments were conducted

46. technology was viewed as a process

47. the technological procedure was to

48. the details of the technological program were presented to

49. choose a technology topic to explore

50. the teacher selected a technological topic

51. students researched technological history

52. the students planned a technological field trip

53. teachers explained the importance of technology

54. the technological steps were detailed

55. students will write papers on technological changes

56. a technology manual was used

57. students found technological resources

58. technology summaries were presented

59. the technology grant provided teachers with

60. technology books were reviewed

61. technology was connected with

62. the value of technology was

63. technology was viewed in relation to

64. technology student groups shared information

65. teachers and students discussed technology issues

66. students kept technology journals

67. technology was encouraged at every stage

68. the technological conclusion was

69. technology captured the student's attention

70. technological questions were developed

71. the idea behind the technology project was

72. technology professionals were consultants for

73. technology research was analyzed

74. students organized technological information

75. changing technology was addressed

76. the purpose of technology was identified

77. the first stage of the technology project involved

78. technological examples were helpful

79. the highlight of the technology department was

80. technological jargon was addressed

81. technology was interpreted by

82. technology was part of the curriculum

83. schools began addressing technological concerns

84. some teachers tried to avoid technology use

85. a survey was given on technology knowledge

86. technology concerns were explained by the teachers

87. students researched technology issues in newspapers

88. the objectives of the technology program were

89. a technology schedule was developed

90. technology subject matter was reviewed

91. the intent of the technology program was to

92. technology responsibility was discussed

93. teachers were assessed on technology knowledge

94. the basics of technology were

95. the technology theme was communicated to

96. feedback was given to the technology unit

97. the technology curriculum was revised

98. technology lessons were developed

99. a technology instructor was hired

100. teachers mentored students in using technology

101. technological research was encouraged

102. technological thinking was enhanced

103. there was a need for another technology teacher

104. technology teachers were in demand

105. the technology lab was obsolete

106. the outdated computer technology was evident

107. up-to-date technology information was important

108. technology changed quickly

109. technology was moving at a rapid pace

110. technological advice was given

111. the technological report was reviewed

112. a technological grant was developed to

113. the technology committee addressed the problem

114. the school planned a technology week

115. technology appealed to the students

116. the technology action plan included

117. dates were discussed for the technology fair

118. vital technology information was debated

119. the newest technology was studied

120. the aim of technology in the school was

121. the technology was too complex for some students

122. technology helped students to construct

123. technological publications were ordered for schools

124. the impact of technology was discussed in groups

125. technological specialists met to develop

126. a final statement was made about the technology mission

127. the technology sequence was presented

128. technology efforts were initiated by

129. the focus of the technology effort was to

130. teachers responded to the technology surge

131. a technology textbook was reviewed

132. the technology program was individualized

133. students shared their thoughts on technology

134. guidelines were developed for the technology center

135. technology activities were closely supervised

136. ways were suggested to evaluate technology activities

137. technological objectives were mastered

138. care of the computer technology lab was discussed

139. long term technology objectives were written

140. technology materials and supplies were ordered

141. technological application is important for

142. students were given technological opportunities to

143. a technological internship was developed

144. problem solving skills were emphasized in technology

145. technology was integrated with

146. the technology framework included

147. technological design developed

148. the technology lab was well organized

149. the technology division was represented by

150. technology vocabulary was introduced

151. there was a resistance to technological change

152. a specific technology plan was identified

153. technology contributed to

154. technology activities were well planned

155. technology progress was recorded

156. students were surveyed on computer technology

157. teachers needed technological support

158. teachers requested technological training

159. a new technological approach was introduced

160. technology was intended to

161. the function of technology is

162. technology meets students needs by

163. technology progress was monitored

164. teachers were unsure of the future of technology

165. technology tutoring was provided

166. the technology program was open to all students

167. teachers need technology assistance

168. technology assignments were given to students

169. students were positively reinforced for using technology

170. each student had a year long technology project

171. technology programs were implemented

172. a technology folder was developed on each student

173. lesson plans included a technology component

174. key technology words were introduced

175. adjustments were made to the technology program

176. the staff developed technology goals for the school

177. additional time was needed for technology

178. technology assignments were developed

179. a list of technology tasks was posted

180. technology was used in all areas of instruction

181. technology access was provided for all students

182. a technology portfolio was submitted

183. technology prizes were awarded to students

184. technology guidelines were helpful for

185. teachers incorporated technology with

186. technology study guides were utilized

187. questioning techniques increased technology interest

188. a technological approach helped in organizing the

189. there were obstacles in the technology area

190. technology was recognized as part of the curriculum

191. technology work samples were kept on the students

192. teachers recapped the technology achievements

193. technology was a flexible part of the curriculum

194. the technology mission statement emphasized

195. the school district had a vision of technology

196. the community cooperated with the school technology program

197. a technology supervisor directed the teachers

198. technology leadership was needed in the district

199. students were given technology learning experiences

200. teachers purchased technology materials and supplies

201. technology was incorporated into the school's improvement plan

202. technology instructional strategies were developed

203. a committee addressed technology decisions

204. parents were involved in technology training

205. parents were trained as technology tutors

206. teachers were suspicious about the technology program

207. technological encouragement is needed

208. computer technology is lacking in some schools

209. high expectations were part of the technology program

210. the teacher's role in technology is

211. teachers demonstrated the use of technology

212. support for the technological unit was provided by

213. technology was explored during in-service training

214. technology possibilities are endless

215. the goals of the school technology program are

216. technology benefits students by

217. technology is significant for

218. technology mistakes were made by teachers

219. technology skills were needed for student job training

220. the growth of technology impacted the schools

221. a technology plan helped organize the teachers

222. there were high goals for the technology department

223. a technology quiz was developed

224. students were accepting of the technology requirements

225. some teachers had negative attitudes toward technology

226. technological information was exchanged

227. teachers shared technological ideas at workshops

228. computer technology connected the schools

229. the school sponsored a technology seminar

230. the school technology program was acknowledged by

231. a technology draft was presented

232. the technology program originated from

233. technology installation was a problem

234. teachers must inventory the technological equipment

235. the technology program was audited

236. the technology department was investigated by

237. an inquiry was made about the technology training

238. technological points were stressed by the

239. technology professions were introduced to the students

240. the students formed technology clubs and organizations

241. a technology fact sheet was given to the students

242. the technology unit cultivated learning

243. technology was articulated by

244. teachers compared the technology materials

245. lesson plans revealed different uses of technology

246. a technology agenda was presented to teachers

247. technology student essays were judged

248. students used technology to create

249. technology inventions were displayed

250. technology comprised a portion of

251. the technology division was responsible for

252. technology was aligned with

253. the scope of technology included

254. the confusion of technology was mentioned

255. technology issues were perplexing to some teachers

256. teachers were misinformed about technology

257. technology was a broad topic

258. technology was amplified in the schools

259. teachers were resourceful with technology

260. each technology unit was unique

261. teachers were overwhelmed by technology

262. grade levels developed their technology units

263. a technology packet was given to teachers

264. the curriculum included a technology emphasis

265. time was allotted for technology training

266. technology was fragmented in the schools

267. technology instruction was divided into sections

268. technology was examined in the past and the present

269. teachers had an individual approach to technology

270. some teachers had to be persuaded to use technology

271. technology was an appropriate part of

272. the technology program was designed to

273. technology procedures were outlined by

274. the principal gave an overview of technology

275. the technology funds were cut

276. funding impacted the success of technology

277. teachers had limited information on technology

278. the practical side of technology was

279. the technology unit was workable

280. teachers made reasonable technology requests

281. the technology plan was feasible

282. the principal arranged the technology in-service training

283. the main goal of technology is

284. technology is important to

285. technology is essential for students to

286. the fundamentals of technology include

287. the technology program was praised

288. progress continued in school technology programs

289. teachers encouraged each other to use technology

290. teacher participation was essential for technology success

291. technology helped teachers establish

292. the direction of technology was

293. technology training was mandatory for teachers

294. students kept a technology notebook

295. technology aimed to

296. the objectives of technology involved

297. teachers accepted the challenges of technology

298. some teachers opposed the use of technology

299. adjustments were made for the technology department

300. technology was correlated with

CHAPTER FIVE

THINGS TEACHERS WOULD LIKE TO KNOW ABOUT TECHNOLOGY

I was attending a staff development day, when the principal announced it was time for the technology portion of the planned program. Some of the teachers at the school had received brand new computers and were not sure how to use them. I must add that with the new computers, teachers were not provided a printer or any software. It was assumed that the teachers would purchase these items out of their personal money. The principal's presentation lasted about ten minutes and basically showed the teachers how to turn on the computer and get the monitor started. The teachers who knew this information quietly laughed at the computer training. However, I observed something different in the older teachers that did not have the technology background. These teachers moved up close as the principal spoke and they were hungry to learn new technological information. These teachers needed the basics and they were thankful for any help they could get to learn technology skills. Unfortunately, ten minutes was all the principal had planned to spend on technology and the rest of the program was devoted to math and science. I can not totally blame the principal for the short presentation because he was not trained in technology and he was just trying to help the teachers get their computers going in the classroom. What I observed that day is that teachers need and want quality technology training that is related to the classroom environment. The following items of this chapter include some things that teachers would like to know about technology in the educational setting:

1. What types of technology are available in the school and the district?

2. What software programs and site licenses does the school have access to use?

3. How do teachers find out about and use the available technology?

4. What is the school's software budget?

5. How is the software budget divided among grade levels?

6. Why are early childhood programs sometimes bumped out of the school's computer and technology program?

7. What computers and technological equipment does the school have in storage?

8. Is there an inventory of the school technology equipment and supplies?

9. What training is available to help teachers improve computer skills?

10. Is there a help-line to answer questions that teachers have about technology?

11. Who are the key resource technology professionals in the district to help teachers?

12. What is the principal's view of technology?

13. How do teacher's use technology to produce student incentives such as stickers, flyers, banners and newsletters?

14. Where do teachers get help in basic computer literacy?

15. How do teachers troubleshoot computers?

16. How do teachers install and download computer software programs?

17. What are some ways teachers can communicate and network together with computers and technology?

18. What is the purpose of a database?

19. How do teachers makes a spreadsheet?

20. How do teachers use computer generated graphics in the classroom?

21. Where do teachers get hands-on technology experience?

22. What technology devices (besides computers) are available for teachers?

23. How can teachers improve word processing skills?

24. What are some of the more advanced features of the computer?

25. Is training provided in the school district for using the Internet?

26. How do teachers download information from various websites?

27. How do teachers use desktop publishing in the classroom with students?

28. What graphic features do computers provide for teachers?

29. How can technology be combined with traditional instructional methods and strategies?

30. Is there help for teachers who have a fear of technology to reach a comfortable level?

31. Where can teachers get a good explanation of hardware and software?

32. What telecommunication programs are available to teachers and students?

33. How can technology make life easier and less stressful for teachers?

34. What record-keeping technology programs could help teachers manage paperwork?

35. How can technology enhance the classroom and school environment?

36. What technology tutorial programs are available to help students with traditional school subjects?

37. How can technology be used to reinforce and supplement the teacher's instruction?

38. What types of technology programs would assist students with homework?

39. How can teachers effectively demonstrate the use of technology to students?

40. What technology instructional games are available to students?

41. How can technology be used to improve reading and math test scores?

42. What student data can be stored in computers?

43. How can teachers get information on computer-based testing?

44. What resources are available through school and district computer labs?

45. Who selects the technology equipment for the school district?

46. Who coordinates the technology services for the district?

47. How can computers be integrated with the school district's established curriculum?

48. Who provides computer maintenance and repair services for the schools?

49. Are demonstration programs available for teachers to test software before it is purchased by the district?

50. What security and safety features are provided on computers in the district?

51. How many students does the computer lab have a capacity to accommodate?

52. Who schedules the computer and technology classes at the school?

53. How much computer and technology training do students receive weekly?

54. Are teachers provided with inservice training on computer lab procedures?

55. How can computers be used to best serve at risk students?

56. What technology techniques would help students functioning below grade level?

57. What resources are available to help teachers when computers and technology malfunction?

58. What computer instructional strategies would help enhance the classroom environment?

59. What interactive technology could be used in the classroom?

60. Is there a reference area in the school or district to locate new and updated technology information?

61. How can the school library be enhanced by computers and technology?

62. How can technology help students learning a new language or a second language?

63. What is multimedia technology?

64. How can teachers obtain multiple copies of software?

65. Does the school have Internet hookups?

66. What kind of technology access and hookups are available through the school?

67. Are technology inservice workshops developed for teachers throughout the year?

68. Who monitors computer and technology equipment checkout and inventory at the school?

69. Where is the software stored for teacher checkout at the school?

70. How can teachers deal with technological change in the classroom?

71. How can teachers use technology for curriculum planning?

72. What are some ways that technology can be used for connecting teachers and students at different schools in joint educational projects?

73. Should teachers invest in technology for their personal use?

74. How can computer chat rooms enhance educational learning?

75. What are some ways teachers can use distance learning technology programs to customize the curriculum?

76. How can schools get connected with universities through technology?

77. How do teachers keep up with new versions of software programs?

78. Why don't teachers have more of a voice in implementing technology programs?

79. How can teachers create their own software educational programs?

80. When are schools going to have more updated computer and technology equipment?

81. Where can teachers find information on Internet educational topics?

82. Are there security systems on classroom computers to prevent student abuse of equipment?

83. How can teachers be trained to connect and install new technology equipment?

84. What are some things that teachers can do to vary teaching strategies with technology in the classroom?

85. Do teachers need district approval for obtaining access to certain websites?

86. What specific technologies can be used in different subject areas?

87. How can teachers help students come up with technological solutions?

88. Are there workshops to help teachers with technological design?

89. Where can teachers find information on technological advances that impact the lives of students?

90. How is technology interrelated with each school subject?

91. What predictions can teachers and students make about technology?

92. Where can teachers find information on technological contributions that have changed society?

93. How can technology be used to help students improve problem solving skills?

94. What types of technology can be combined to enhance the curriculum?

95. Can technology be used to help students improve comprehension skills?

96. What ways can technology be used to help students improve comprehension skills?

97. What ways can technology be utilized to help teachers develop timelines and sequence historical events?

98. How can technology be used to demonstrate solutions to real-world problems?

99. Are there specific technology programs that would help improve reading, writing and math skills?

100. Where can teachers find examples of technology devices that save time in the real world?

101. How can technology be used in the classroom to increase geographical awareness?

102. What are some ways teachers and students can collect data with technology?

103. How can technology be utilized to display student work?

104. What are some ways teachers can assess and test technological abilities in their students?

105. When is it appropriate to use technology to help with conflict resolutions?

106. What are some things teachers can do to encourage technological awareness with students?

107. Can technology be used in school programs such as health and counseling offices to reach more students?

108. When is it appropriate to use technology in small group instruction?

109. How can technology be modified to help students with special needs?

110. Who can help implement and consult with teachers on establishing technological goals?

111. Can technology save teachers time in weekly lesson plan preparation?

112. Is computer training necessary for all students?

113. Is the technology in the school in alignment with the school's educational mission and goals?

114. Do teachers have the training to teach technology skills at the mastery level?

115. What type of district leadership is available to assist teachers with technology information?

116. How can technology be adapted for students to work independently in task oriented activities?

117. When is it important to include parents in the school technology training?

118. What is the teacher's supervisory responsibility when working with students and technological devices?

119. Has the school district developed guidelines to address improper use of computers and technology?

120. What are the rights and responsibilities of students and teachers when using technology in the schools?

121. Is there a filtering system to limit student access to unsuitable material?

122. Does the school district have a committee or board to address technological problems and concerns?

123. Does the school district provide enough training for teachers to proficiently instruct technology?

124. Are there instructional strategists who evaluate the usefulness of software in relation to the curriculum?

125. Are all teachers provided with access to the Internet and an email address for professional use?

126. Does the district have guidelines to address ethical issues related to computer and technology use?

127. How can teacher technology training be improved and become more teacher friendly?

128. Do classrooms have enough storage for computer books and software?

129. Is there a school audit system to inventory and audit technology equipment?

130. Do teachers have control over their computers and methods of teaching technology?

131. What copyright issues impact teachers as they use and copy software?

132. Does the school district provide technology support to assist teachers?

133. Are teachers involved in the software selection process of the school district?

134. What information is provided to teachers on the main features of the Internet?

135. Has the school district prepared easy teacher resource guides about available Internet information?

136. Are teachers asked to be consultants or trainers for technological companies?

137. Does the school district's technology program provided enrichment for gifted and talented students?

138. Can teachers earn advanced degrees by taking online college courses?

139. How much technology training is provided for teachers during a school year?

140. What are the state requirements for teachers to obtain a technology endorsement?

141. Where can teachers find out about school related technology jobs?

142. Are all classrooms wired with computer hookups?

143. Does the school's technology program have a component to help learning disabled students?

144. Is the technology equipment divided equitably for at risk schools and more affluent schools?

145. Are teachers kept aware of current research that involves students and technology?

146. Is there any special assistance to help teachers resistant to technological training?

147. Are teachers familiar with creative ways to enhance student interest in technology?

148. How can classrooms be modified to provide optical technological educational support for students?

149. Has the school district developed criteria for evaluating technology learning programs?

150. What evaluation techniques are used by the district to ensure effective technology programs?

151. How are school districts keeping up with emerging technology?

152. What is the district's role and attitude about technology in the classroom?

153. How do teachers address principals who are reluctant about technological change?

154. Do school districts provide support and technology training for teachers at the beginning and advanced levels of experience?

155. Is technology used across the school curriculum?

156. How must teachers change their teaching styles to incorporate technology in the classroom?

157. How can technology be used by teachers making student assessments?

158. Do teachers have assistance in obtaining the skills to locate technological information for the classroom?

159. Are teachers trained to help students critically evaluate technological information?

160. Does the school district provide enough hands on experience for teachers to feel competent using technology?

161. Are teachers given enough release time to practice and maintain technology skills after they attend inservice workshops?

162. Are opportunities provided for teachers to discuss and share technological concerns?

163. Is the school district actively submitting grant proposals for teacher technological training and support?

164. When new technological equipment arrives in a school, are teachers inserviced on how to use it?

165. Does the school district have a plan of how technology is implemented in the schools?

166. Are teachers and support staff at all levels participating in technological training?

167. Are stolen computers and technological equipment replaced quickly so that the student's learning is not hindered?

168. Do teachers have access to the technology they have been trained to use?

169. Are opportunities provided for teachers who want advanced technological training?

170. What incentives do school districts provided to encourage teachers to participate in technological training?

171. How can teachers use world wide web discussion groups?

172. What technology related activities would help students improve leadership skills?

173. How can technology help teachers with classroom management and discipline issues?

174. Can technology help students become more organized and task oriented?

175. What are some ways the structure and format of the class change by using technology?

176. What training is provided for teachers to learn how to demonstrate technology use?

177. How are textbooks incorporated with the use of technology in the classroom?

178. Is there a directory of classroom assignments that are completed through the use of technology?

179. Are students aware of the technology available in the school?

180. Does the school promote and encourage technology activities for staff and students?

181. Have teachers been surveyed about their attitudes and experiences related to technology?

182. Are there guidelines for storing and arranging technology equipment in the classrooms?

183. Should technology be more student centered or teacher centered in the classroom environment?

184. How can time management be implemented with the use of technology in the classroom?

185. How can student discussions be stimulated through the use of technology?

186. Does the teacher become more of a facilitator when technology is used in the classroom?

187. Are there checkpoints or cautions teachers should know when using technology?

188. Should technology be taught as individualized instruction to students?

189. What opportunities are available to use technology with cross-age and peer instruction?

190. How can technology be used prior to a field trip to provide an orientation to students?

191. What are some good technological field trips for students?

192. What questioning techniques work well with the use of technology in the classroom?

193. Can teacher lectures still be used with technology?

194. What challenges do teachers face using technology in special education settings?

195. How can technology be used to help students with language and speech disorders or impairments?

196. What are some ways to design portfolio assessments with technology?

197. How do the students respond to using technology in the classroom?

198. What are some weaknesses of using technology in the classroom?

199. How can technology be used to improve the overall classroom environment and the lives of students?

200. Will technology presented in the classroom help change the lives of students in a positive way?

IDENTIFY TECHNOLOGY GOALS IN THE SCHOOL SETTING

Teachers are sometimes confused about technology because they are unsure about district, school and personal technology goals. Complete the following items on technology goals:

Describe the school district's technology mission and goal.
1.

2.

3.

List the goals of your school for technology inclusion.
1.

2.

3.

Describe the school's department or grade level goals for implementing technology.
1.

2.

3.

Relate your personal goals for including technology in the classroom.
1.

2.

3.

TEACHERS INTEREST INVENTORY USING TECHNOLOGY

Answer the following questions honestly about your interest as a teacher in technology and share in pairs or discussion groups:

1. How do you feel about using technology in the classroom setting?

2. What types of technology do you use in your classroom?

3. How would you describe the technical support and assistance the school district provides to teachers?

4. What is your reaction to technological change in our society?

5. What is your comfort level with using technology in the classroom?

6. How would you describe the equipment available to you to utilize technology at your school?

7. What are some barriers you find in implementing the use of technology in your classroom?

8. How would you describe the student's view of technology in your classroom?

9. How would you describe the strengths of your school's technology program?

TEACHER TRAINING
TECHNOLOGICAL SURVEY

Please indicate below with a check mark your need for training in the following areas:

	I really need training in this area.	I can use some assistance in this area.	I do not need training in this area.
1. Start up assistance in hooking up computers and technology equipment.			
2. Demonstration of basic tasks using operating systems with computers.			
3. Information on how to integrate software with daily lesson plans and curriculum.			
4. Hands-on inservice training to practice and develop technology skills and confidence.			
5. Consultation with experts to answer questions about the use of technology equipment.			
6. Training sessions on selecting appropriate educational software.			
7. Advice and help in creating effective technology classroom activities.			
8. Information and outlines for developing database programs, grading programs and spreadsheets.			
9. Technological training for upgrades and new advancements in technology.			
10. Demonstrations on how to establish multi-school technology communications.			

FOUR KEYS TO SUCCESSFUL TEACHER TECHNOLOGY PROGRAMS

Schools who desire to have successful technology programs must consider four keys when developing programs with teachers and staff:

1. QUALITY TECHNOLOGY TRAINING

Teachers have been going to workshops, staff development days and training sessions for years. They have heard both exciting and well-organized speakers, as well as stuffy and boring presentations. I remember hearing a talk from a principal who emphasized that this technology stuff was a "passing fad" and that the district was spending money on it now, but he thought is would go away in a few years. When the technological workshop was presented it did not seem sincere and the little training that teachers received was far from adequate. Teachers need quality training from dedicated professionals who believe in the benefits of technology in the classroom and who are up-to-date with the latest technological information.

2. SUPPORT AND CONSULTATION

A teacher colleague shared with me that the technology strategist at his school was totally stressed out. The new computers had arrived the first month of school and he was bombarded with questions from teachers. The 53 teachers wanted to know everything about turning on and hooking up the computers. Teachers need ongoing consultation and support or the technology will become stored and pushed in the corner cabinet.

3. AVAILABLE EQUIPMENT AND SOFTWARE

Teachers need the equipment to use once they are trained to operate it. I have had so much training on computers and I leave the workshop only to find that in a few weeks I have forgotten all the information that I was introduced to in the workshop. The technology equipment was not available to practice and fine tune my skills. The same principle holds true with software. If teachers are given computers with no software it will set idle in their classrooms. I reviewed a school plan once and found the school's software budget was five hundred dollars for a staff of thirty teachers. It does not take an expert in accounting to calculate that the teachers get peanuts to purchase software for the classroom. Districts must appropriate funds for equipment and software if they want teachers to enhance skills and teach the technological information to students in an effective and successful learning environment.

4. TEACHER INCENTIVES FOR TECHNOLOGY USE

Many school environments constantly emphasize incentive programs for students, but do nothing to encourage teachers. There are many incentive programs that could be developed to encourage teachers to use technology in the classroom.

The following list is a few examples of how teachers can be encouraged and rewarded for technology use:

Release time one day a month for technology training and support.

Free educational software for teachers who share innovative ideas on using technology.

Certificates of recognition for outstanding lesson plans that incorporate technological use.

Give technology books as door prizes during technology training sessions.

A classroom computer for teachers who develop three outstanding class lessons with a technology emphasis to share with other teachers.

Opportunities to attend technology conferences for teachers who have logged 100 hours of computer use in the classroom.

VARIABLES THAT IMPACT TECHNOLOGY IN THE SCHOOLS

* PRIORITY OF TECHNOLOGY

Some schools place technology as a high prioity, while other schools put it low on the list of school activities. Basically, some schools are technologically friendly, while others put it on the back burner.

* TRAINING PROVIDED TO TEACHERS

There is a great disparity in the amount of technology training that teachers receive from schools. For example, my husband taught in a middle school and was constantly attending technology inservice training and present at technology conferences. The elementary school that I taught at for five years seldom had any training in technology.

* ATTITUDES OF ADMINISTRATORS AND TEACHERS

Some administrators and teachers are reluctant to change the things they have been doing in the classroom. There are a variety of reasons for this reluctance. Some teachers and administrators are afraid of change, while others think it is a waste of time and money. Attitudes can play a major role in how a school technology program is implemented.

* TECHNOLOGY LEADERSHIP

One variable observed in how technology is implemented at a school is the leadership qualities of the person in charge of the technology program. An educational technology specialist or department chair with good organizational and delegation skills will reach more teachers with technology information than someone who lacks the leadership abilities and communication skills to contact the teachers.

WHAT TEACHERS WANT

- ◆ TO FEEL COMFORTABLE WITH TECHNOLOGY IN THE CLASSROOM

- ◆ TO MOTIVATE STUDENTS TO ENJOY LEARNING WITH TECHNOLOGY

- ◆ TO PROVIDE A VARIETY OF LEARNING ACTIVITIES WITH TECHNOLOGY IN THE CLASSROOM

- ◆ TO IMPROVE STUDENT'S PROBLEM-SOLVING SKILLS USING TECHNOLOGY

- ◆ TO IMPLEMENT TECHNOLOGY PROGRAMS THAT CAN REACH STUDENTS AT VARIOUS ABILITY LEVELS

- ◆ TO PROVIDE ENRICHING TECHNOLOGY EXPERIENCES THAT WILL IMPROVE THE QUALITY OF LIFE FOR STUDENTS

BIBLIOGRAPHY

To help teachers gain a broader perspective on technology issues, I recommend the following books for reading:

Ardis, Susan B. *Library Without Walls: Plug In and Go.* Washington, DC: Special Libraries Association, 1994.

Blake, Virgil P. and Tjouman, Renee, (Eds.). *Information Literacies for the Twenty-First Century.* Boston, MA: G.K. Hall and Company, 1990.

Bunch, Bryan and Hellemans, Alexander. *The Timetables of Technology: A Chronology of the Most Important People and Events in the History of Technology.* New York, NY: Simon and Schuster, 1993.

Lewis, H.W. *Technological Risk.* New York, NY: W. W. Norton and Company, 1990.

MacKenzic, Donald and Wajcman, Judy (Eds.). *The Social Shaping of Technology.* Philadelphia, PA: Open University Press, 1985.

Nelson, Nancy Merlin. *Technology for the 90's: Microcomputers in Libraries.* Westport, CT: Meckler, 1989.

Postman, Neil. *Technopoly: The Surrender of Culture to Technology.* New York, NY: Alfred A. Knopf, 1992.

Tenner, Edward. *Why Things Bite Back: Technology and the Revenge of Unintended Consequences.* New York, NY: Alfred A. Knopf, 1996.

SUBJECT INDEX

ABOUT THE AUTHOR

Susan Louise Peterson has professional experiences as a human relations consultant, a college professor, and a teacher of at-risk students in the public schools. She is the author of several books in the education and social science areas. Her book credits through International Scholar's Publications include: *The Educator's Phrase Book,* and *At-Risk Students: Tools for Teaching in Problem Settings.*